# PEOPLES OF THE ANCIENT WORLD

# Life in Ancient Mesoamerica

Lynn Peppas

Crabtree Publishing Company

www.crabtreebooks.com

# Crabtree Publishing Company

www.crabtreebooks.com

# For Neil MacIntyre

Coordinating editor: Ellen Rodger
Project editor: Sean Charlebois
Editors: Rachel Eagen, Carrie Gleason, Adrianna Morganelli
Production coordinator: Rosie Gowsell
Production assistance: Samara Parent
Scanning technician: Arlene Arch-Wilson
Photo research: Allison Napier
Art director: Rob MacGregor

Project management assistance:
Media Projects, Inc.
Carter Smith
Pat Smith
Laura Smyth
Aimee Kraus
Michael Greenhut

Consultants: Dr. Sandra Noble, Executive Director, Foundation for the Advancement of Mesoamerican Studies, Florida

Barbara Richman, Farragut Middle School, Hastings-on-Hudson, NY

Photographs: Art Resource, NY: p. 24, p. 29; Bettmann/CORBIS: p. 12; Bodleian Library: p. 27; Donne Bryant/Art Resource, NY: p. 29; Jack Fields/CORBIS: p. 14; Mary Evans Picture Library: p. 20; ET Archive: p. 11, p. 20, p. 21, p. 27; Werner Forman/CORBIS: p. 28; Werner Forman/Art Resource, NY: p. 15, p. 19, p. 24; Fotosearch: p. 13, p. 19; Getty Images: p. 17, p. 30; Kimbell Art Museum/CORBIS: p. 8; Erich Lessing/Art Resource, NY: p. 4, p. 25; Library of Congress: p. 31; David Muench/CORBIS: p. 7; Gianni Dagli Orti/CORBIS: p. 3, p. 9, p. 12, p. 13, p. 17, p. 26; Carl & Ann Purcell/CORBIS: p. 21; Roger Ressmeyer/CORBIS: p. 7; Scala/Art Resource, NY: p. 9; Schalkwijk/Art Resource, NY: p. 11; Superstock: p. 10

Illustrations: James Burmester: p. 16; Crabtree Publishing: p. 16; Roman Goforth: p. 1, p. 18; Rose Gowsell: p. 5; Robert McGregor: pp. 4–5 (timeline), p. 6, p. 30

Cartography: Jim Chernishenko: p. 6

Cover: Detail from Mayan carving, Presentation of the Jaguar Mask, from between 350 A.D. and 900 A.D.

Title page: An Aztec temple built in the city of Tenochtitlán. It served as a holy site.

## Crabtree Publishing Company

www.crabtreebooks.com          1-800-387-7650

Cataloging-in-Publication data

Peppas, Lynn.
    Life in ancient Mesoamerica / written by Lynn Peppas.
       p. cm. -- (Peoples of the ancient world)
    Includes index.
    ISBN 0-7787-2039-X (rlb) -- ISBN 0-7787-2069-1 (pbk)
    1. Indians of Mexico--Antiquities. 2. Indians of Mexico--History. 3. Indians of Mexico--Social life and customs. 4. Mexico--Social life and customs. 5. Mexico--Antiquities. I. Title. II. Series.
    F1219.P385 2005
    972'.01--dc22
                                      2004013069
                                      LC

**Published in the United States**
PMB 16A
350 Fifth Ave.
Suite 3308
New York, NY
10118

**Published in Canada**
616 Welland Ave.
St. Catharines
Ontario, Canada
L2M 5V6

**Published in the United Kingdom**
73 Lime Walk
Headington
Oxford
OX3 7AD
United Kingdom

**Published in Australia**
386 Mt. Alexander Rd.
Ascot Vale (Melbourne)
V1C 3032

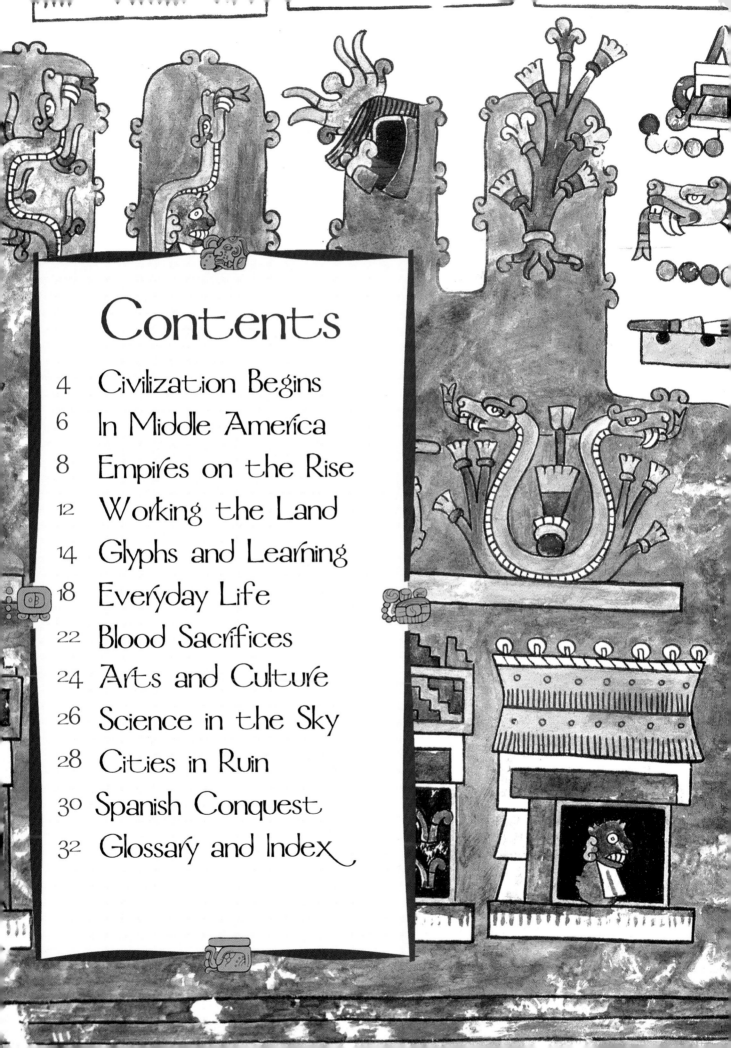

# Contents

4   Civilization Begins

6   In Middle America

8   Empires on the Rise

12   Working the Land

14   Glyphs and Learning

18   Everyday Life

22   Blood Sacrifices

24   Arts and Culture

26   Science in the Sky

28   Cities in Ruin

30   Spanish Conquest

32   Glossary and Index

# Civilization Begins

About 50,000 years ago, the first peoples arrived in the Americas from Asia. At that time a land bridge connected the two continents where the Bering Strait is today. The descendants of these peoples spread south and reached Mesoamerica, or the land between North and South America, about 10,000 years ago. Over thousands of years, the Olmec, Maya, and Aztec peoples each made stunning achievements.

## Early Settlements

The earliest Mesoamerican settlements formed in the lowlands along the Pacific coast around 1500 B.C. In small villages of about a dozen homes, Mesoamericans grew a corn called maize, fished, and collected oysters, clams, and turtles from the nearby lagoons and **estuaries**. In the highlands, where the **climate** was much drier, villagers traded goods in order to survive.

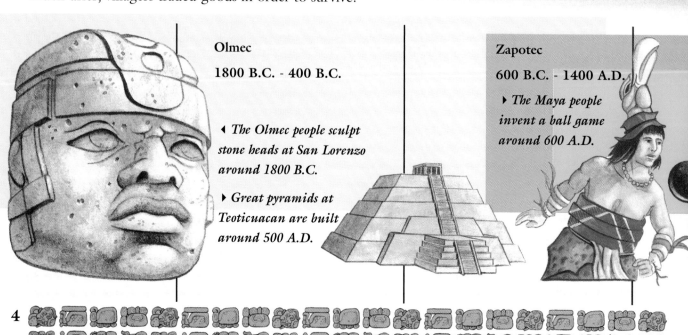

**Olmec**

1800 B.C. - 400 B.C.

◀ *The Olmec people sculpt stone heads at San Lorenzo around 1800 B.C.*

▶ *Great pyramids at Teoticuacan are built around 500 A.D.*

**Zapotec**

600 B.C. - 1400 A.D.

▶ *The Maya people invent a ball game around 600 A.D.*

## Achievements

The first civilization was the Olmec, who settled on the Gulf of Mexico's coast in about 1500 B.C. The most recent civilization was the Aztec, who were **conquered** by Spanish explorers in about 1500 A.D. In a period of 3,000 years, the Olmec, Aztec, Maya, and other peoples such as the Toltec and Zapotec, charted the skies to tell time and built enormous pyramids in which they worshiped their gods.

# What is a "civilization?"

Most historians agree that a civilization is a group of people that shares common languages, some form of writing, advanced technology and science, and systems of government and religion.

◄ *The great pyramid in Chichén Itzá, Mexico, was built by the Maya as a place to perform religious ceremonies.*

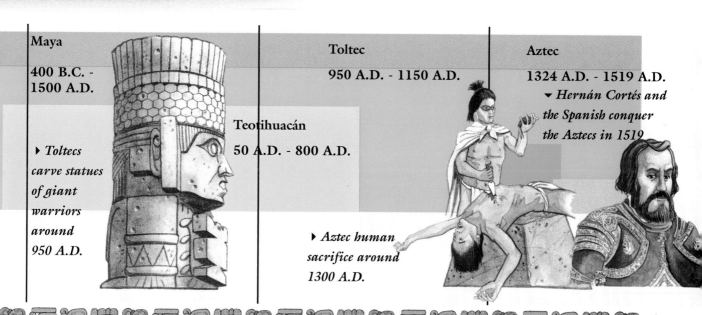

**Maya**

400 B.C. - 1500 A.D.

▶ *Toltecs carve statues of giant warriors around 950 A.D.*

**Toltec**

950 A.D. - 1150 A.D.

Teotihuacán

50 A.D. - 800 A.D.

▶ *Aztec human sacrifice around 1300 A.D.*

**Aztec**

1324 A.D. - 1519 A.D.

▼ *Hernán Cortés and the Spanish conquer the Aztecs in 1519*

# In Middle America

**Ancient Mesoamerica was located where the countries of southern Mexico, Belize, Guatemala, Honduras, El Salvador, Nicaragua, Costa Rica, and Panama are today. Mesoamerica has tropical forests and snow-capped volcanoes, mountains, deserts, and swamplands. The land's diversity was important to the development of the Olmec, Maya, and Aztec civilizations.**

## Highlands and Lowlands

The peoples of Mesoamerica lived in the highlands, lowlands, and coastal plains between the Gulf of Mexico and the Pacific Ocean. The Olmec heartland hugged the Gulf of Mexico on the Gulf Coast and dipped slightly into the **isthmus** of Tehuantepec. The Maya branched out over a broader area that included the Yucatán **peninsula** of Mexico, Belize, parts of Guatemala, and

northern areas of Honduras and El Salvador. The Aztec lived in the Valley of Mexico, between the Sierra Madre Occidental and the Sierra Madre Oriental mountain ranges.

▼ *The word mesoamerica means "between Americas."*

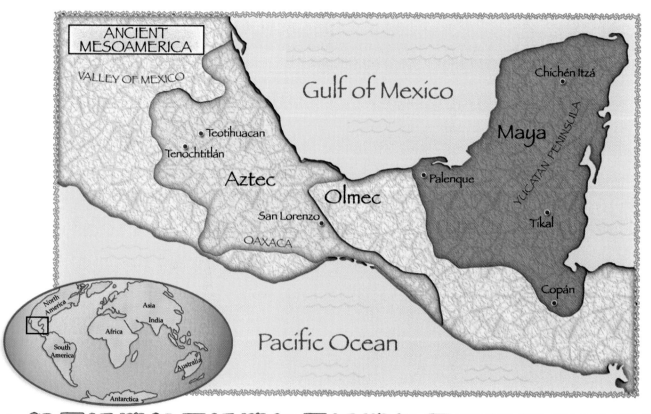

▼ *The maguey plant was used to make a fermented drink called pulque.*

## Vegetation

In the southwest, mountain slopes teemed with lush forests of oak trees. Drier conditions in the north created forests of scrub oak and maguey trees. The ancient Mesoamericans found many uses for the plants around them, especially the maguey plant that grew in the desert regions of central Mexico. They used the maguey's sap to make medicine and soap. Its tough fibers were used to make brushes, rope, and heavy woven fabric used for carrying babies and food.

## Wildlife

Mesoamerica's largest wildcat, the jaguar, lived and hunted in the **dense**, tropical forests and swampy marshes. Jaguars are fierce **carnivores** that are not afraid of humans. To Mesoamericans, jaguars had special meaning. The jaguar was thought of as the king of nature. In sculpture and paintings, the Olmec people often combined the jaguar with the human form.

▶ *Rulers often wore jaguar skins during religious ceremonies as a symbol of their power.*

▲ *The many volcanoes in Mesoamerica produced ash and lava as well as obsidian, a glass formed when lava cools quickly. Obsidian was used to make tools for cutting.*

## Volcanoes

Ancient Mesoamericans had great respect for mountains and volcanoes. The people built towering temples for religious celebrations that were pyramid-shaped to resemble mountains. Volcanoes spewed rocks, such as obsidian and basalt. The Olmec people sculpted colossal stone heads from the dark, volcanic rock basalt.

# Empires on the Rise

**Mesoamericans did not have a single government. The Olmec, Maya, and Aztec each had their own communities, or city-states. A city-state had a ruler, and each ruler was treated like a god. Sometimes city-states fought other city-states and created** empires. **Some city-states joined together in** alliances **to protect themselves from conquerors.**

## Olmec City-States

The Olmecs created the first civilization in Mesoamerica. The Olmecs were **nomadic** hunters who settled into farming communities in the lowland areas near the Gulf of Mexico and the central valley highlands around 1200 B.C. The Olmec people built city-states with grand pyramid-shaped temples in the center that were used for religious ceremonies. They were ruled by governors, called Ku, and kings, called Tu. Olmec rulers lived in the cities while everyone else lived outside the city. Olmec rulers also served as religious leaders and grew very powerful over the city-states and the surrounding area.

## Maya City-States

The Maya civilization reached its peak between 250 A.D. and 900 A.D. The Maya built a kingdom of at least 50 city-states. Each city-state was made up of a large urban center and the surrounding farming communities. The size of a Maya city-state was usually about the distance a person could walk in a day. The urban center had pyramids, temples, and great monuments, which were lined up with the sun, moon, and stars.

▲ *Mesoamerican rulers were treated as though they were gods. In this sculpture from a temple, a Maya king is presented with slaves .*

## Rivals

Maya city-states were not united with each other. The city-states of Tikal and Calakmul were more powerful than the others and controlled smaller city-states. City-states defeated in war had to pay tribute to their conquerors with precious items such as quetzal feathers, cocoa beans, and fine cloth. Quetzal feathers come from a tropical bird and were worn on the headdresses of royals. Cocoa beans were used to make chocolate, which was highly prized by ancient Mesoamericans.

▲ *In this painting from a Maya temple, a great battle is being fought.*

## Maya Rulers

A king ruled each Maya city-state. The king's power was handed down to first-born boys on the father's side. The Maya believed a king had special powers to communicate with the gods. Maya kings wore elaborate clothing and headdresses representing animals to identify them as gods. Kings negotiated trading alliances, maintained the business of the state, and organized construction projects. The king planned military battles to expand and defend a city's territory and capture prisoners for **sacrifice** to the gods.

### Pacal of Palenque

The best known Maya king was Lord Pacal who lived in the city of Palenque between 603 A.D. and 683 A.D. Palenque flourished under the rule of Pacal. Great palaces were built and decorated with **stucco** paintings that depicted the rulers and their families.

◀ *The hairstyle of this stucco head of Pacal looks like maize, or corn leaves, to connect him with the Maize god.*

## The Aztec

The Aztec were a warrior-like group that settled on a snake-inhabited island in the Valley of Mexico's Lake Texcoco in the early 1100s A.D. The neighboring peoples hoped that the rattlesnakes on the island would force the Aztec to leave, but the Aztecs were determined to stay and developed new recipes for rattlesnake meat. For nearly 400 years, the Aztec ruled the region from their mighty city of Tenochtitlán, which they built on the island. Spanish soldiers who arrived in Tenochtitlán destroyed the Aztecs in the early 1500s.

## Aztec Empire: The Triple Alliance

The Aztec empire was tied together through royal and **noble** marriages. Aztec nobles married their sons and daughters to members of other noble families to create alliances. Children of royalty in conquered states were all educated at Tenochtitlán, so royal children all knew one another. As Tenochtitlán grew and prospered, the citizens of the nearby city of Tepanec began to fear that the Aztec would conquer them. To prevent this, they killed the Aztec king. In retaliation, Tlacaelel, a brutal but brilliant Aztec military commander, defeated the Tepanec people. His uncle, Itzcoatl, also called the Obsidian Serpent, then made Tenochtitlán an ally with the cities of Texcoco and Tlacopan. This Triple Alliance of Aztec cities began conquering smaller, surrounding city-states until it controlled most of what is now central Mexico.

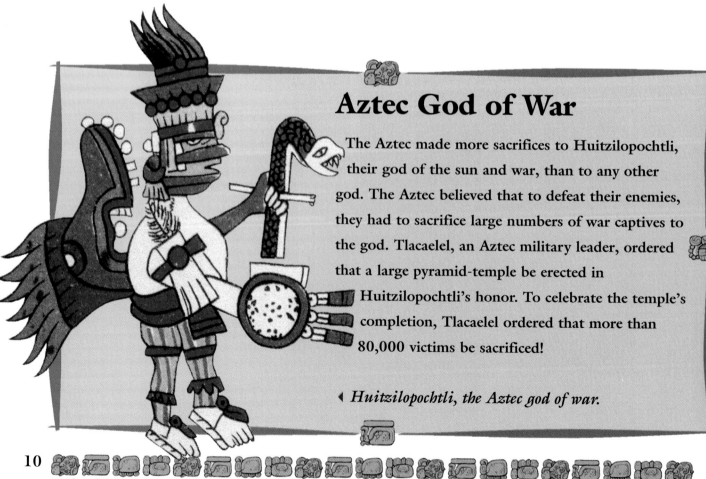

# Aztec God of War

The Aztec made more sacrifices to Huitzilopochtli, their god of the sun and war, than to any other god. The Aztec believed that to defeat their enemies, they had to sacrifice large numbers of war captives to the god. Tlacaelel, an Aztec military leader, ordered that a large pyramid-temple be erected in Huitzilopochtli's honor. To celebrate the temple's completion, Tlacaelel ordered that more than 80,000 victims be sacrificed!

◄ *Huitzilopochtli, the Aztec god of war.*

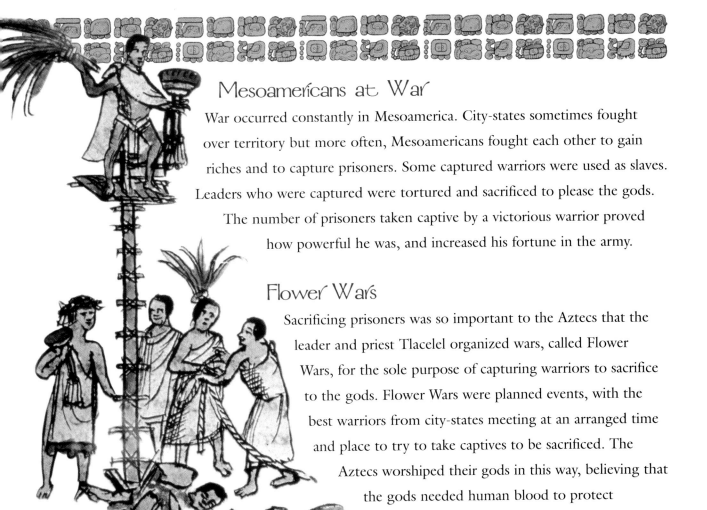

## Mesoamericans at War

War occurred constantly in Mesoamerica. City-states sometimes fought over territory but more often, Mesoamericans fought each other to gain riches and to capture prisoners. Some captured warriors were used as slaves. Leaders who were captured were tortured and sacrificed to please the gods. The number of prisoners taken captive by a victorious warrior proved how powerful he was, and increased his fortune in the army.

## Flower Wars

Sacrificing prisoners was so important to the Aztecs that the leader and priest Tlacelel organized wars, called Flower Wars, for the sole purpose of capturing warriors to sacrifice to the gods. Flower Wars were planned events, with the best warriors from city-states meeting at an arranged time and place to try to take captives to be sacrificed. The Aztecs worshiped their gods in this way, believing that the gods needed human blood to protect the universe.

▲ *The Aztecs battled with their enemies and took many prisoners in the Flower Wars. The real goal of the the Flower Wars was not war, but to take prisoners that the Aztecs could sacrifice to their gods.*

▼ *The Aztec capital of Tenochtitlán was located on a marshy island in the middle of Lake Texcoco in central Mexico. Today, Mexico City sits on the former site of Tenochtitlán.*

# Working the Land

**Around 1800 B.C., Mesoamericans began to settle in small communities. As settlements grew larger, new methods of farming were developed to feed the growing population. People in different parts of Mesoamerica grew different crops, so trade between settlements was necessary.**

## Farming in the Rainforests

To clear rainforest land to grow crops, Mesoamericans used a method called "slash and burn," or *milpa* farming. Farmers cut a tree's bark in a circle around the trunk to kill it. Branches were then cut off and left at the tree's base. After the tree dried out, a fire was set to burn away the vegetation. The ash from the burned trees and vegetation **fertilized** the ground and made the soil good for growing food.

▸ *An Aztec farmer harvests amaranth, an ancient grain that was used to make flour.*

## Floating Gardens

Marshy areas were too wet for *milpa* farming, so Mesoamericans built raised fields, or floating gardens, called *chinampas*. Soil was dug from the surrounding area and piled up to form the banks of a **canal**. Wooden stakes were hammered into the ground to reinforce the canal's banks. Trees were planted around the banks and their roots kept the sides of the canal from being washed away.

◂ **Chinampas** *were built by piling mud on a frame of woven reeds.*

## Trade

Mesoamerican city-states could not survive on what they grew for themselves. Some regions that were good for growing certain crops needed to trade with other regions to get building materials for temples. Trade between neighbors was necessary for the city-states to flourish. In the Aztec city of Tenochtitlán, there were markets every five days where merchants sold food, weapons, and clothing. Some Aztec merchants, called *pochteca*, traveled great distances to trade textiles, clothing, and stone knives with other Mesoamerican peoples.

## Delivering the Goods

Mesoamericans did not have the wheel, or pack animals such as oxen, horses, or donkeys. Food and household items that were being traded had to be carried over land using a backpack called a tumpline. A tumpline rested on a person's back and was secured to the forehead by a headband.

▲ *Aztec workers store amaranth grain in large vessels which were used to carry the grain to markets.*

# Money Grown on Trees

Cocoa beans, which come from pods harvested from the cacao tree, were used as money by the Maya and the Aztecs. Cocoa beans were valuable because they were difficult to grow. The delicate cacao trees grew only in shady areas with high **humidity**. Once allowed to dry in the sun, the valuable beans were easy to carry, so used as money. They were also ground and used in a drink in religious ceremonies.

# Glyphs and Learning

**Mesoamericans invented their own language and writing system. The Maya and the Aztecs created writing systems of hieroglyphs, a number system, and a calendar that was very accurate.**

## Sign Language

Recording with hieroglyphic symbols began with the Olmec, but it was the Maya who developed an entire language. The Maya used a familiar picture, or glyph, that **symbolized** an entire word. The Maya also invented an alphabet that helped them sound out a word when there was not a glyph to represent it. The Aztecs also used glyphs, but unlike the Maya, did not have an alphabet.

## Translating

In the last 100 years, **archaeologists** have learned how to read some Maya glyphs by studying three surviving Maya manuscripts, called codices. Each manuscript is full of stories about which days are best for planting maize, hunting, or going into battle. The codices have allowed archaeologists to identify glyphs for a number of the Maya gods and understand some of their **astronomical** and mathematical calculations.

▶ *This stone pillar, or stele, in Tikal, Guatemala, depicts ancient Maya glyphs.*

## Book Making

Ancient Mesoamericans made folding-screen books with pages made from either deerskin or bark paper. These manuscripts were huge compared to the size of modern books. The Dresden Codex is a Maya book of astronomy that is 74 pages long and eleven feet (three meters) wide when laid out flat. The Maya used mostly bark paper for their books. To make the paper, they soaked the inner bark of trees in water to soften the wood. The bark was then beaten with stones, or a wooden mallet, until smooth. The soft, flat bark was **whitewashed** and painted by scribes. Scribes were men and women skilled in the art of writing and reading glyphs.

▼ *An Aztec codex, or book, was sometimes painted on parchment made from animal skin. Aztec scribes recorded religious stories, their people's history, and even weather forecasts in books.*

# Creation Stories

The greatest stories told throughout Mesoamerica were those from a book called Popol Vuh. Popol Vuh begins with the story of creation, and includes legends of superhero ball-playing twins Hunahpn and Xbalanque. Popul Vuh was written in hieroglyphs by the Maya, but was destroyed by Spanish priests who burned all books after they landed in Mesoamerica in 1519. In 1558, a Mayan who had learned to write using Latin letters recorded the stories from Popol Vuh once again. The book was kept and forgotten in a church in Guatemala for over 100 years. It has since been found and translated into many languages.

## Mayan Math

In Mayan math, there were three symbols to represent numbers. A dot represented one, a bar meant five, and a symbol that looked like a sea shell stood for zero. The symbols were arranged vertically to make larger numbers and arranged from bottom to top. Merchants used the counting system when tallying sums during trade. Math was also used to plan construction of buildings and in astronomy to help figure out dates and times.

A second system of writing numbers was also used. Instead of dots and bars, heads of gods were carved to represent the numbers from one through twelve.

## Math Sums

**Can you do Mayan math? By following the legend shown below left, guess what the sums are below.**

• + = =

•• + ••• =

••• + • =

*(Answers: 16, 20, 24)*

▼ *In the system of writing numbers represented by the heads of gods, more facial features were added for bigger numbers.*

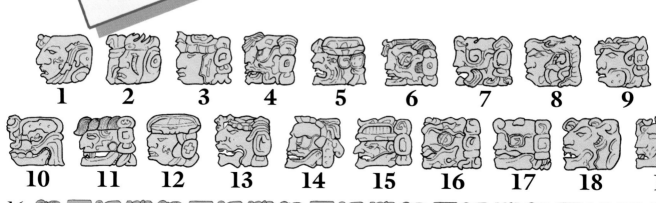

1   2   3   4   5   6   7   8   9

10   11   12   13   14   15   16   17   18   19

## Short Months

The Maya and Aztecs developed complex calendars to measure time. Each month had 20 days and there were two calendar years, one with 260 days and one with 365 days. The two calendars **coincided** every 52 years. This point in time was important to the ancient Mesoamericans. The Maya feared that the sky would fall or that the world might end if the gods were not satisfied. The Aztec marked the 52-year point with the New Fire Festival that lasted twelve days. During the festival there was fasting and human sacrifice.

## Fortune-Telling Machines

The 260-day calendar moved in a repeating cycle. The calendar was used to predict the future, to name babies, and to choose lucky dates for battles and marriages, building houses, or sowing crops. Each day had its own god and good or bad fortune associated with it. The repeating cycle of 20 days has been compared to an endless fortune-telling machine.

The 365-day calendar had eighteen months of 20 days each. It was based on the **solar** cycle. For the Maya, there was an unlucky five-day period at the end of the calendar. For the Aztecs, these five "days of nothing" were festival days when people wore their best clothes and took part in dancing and singing. This was also the time when priests performed sacrifices.

▲ *The circular Aztec calendar was used by priests to remember religious festivals.*

◄ *The Aztecs used signs they saw in the sky to predict disasters. A comet appeared just before the Spanish conquered the Aztecs.*

# Everyday Life

**Ancient Mesoamerican art depicts what life was like for rulers, priests, and nobles. The ruling elite formed a very small part of Mesoamerican civilization, and daily life depended on ordinary people doing backbreaking work such as farming, building temples, and fighting wars. The way people lived depended on their position and role in society.**

## ◄ Emperors

Usually, a king or chief priest was the most important figure in society. For the Aztecs, an even more powerful ruler, called an emperor, was required to govern the three city-states of Tenochtitlán, Texcoco, and Tlacopan.

## Rulers ▼

In Mesoamerican society, the chief priest was also the king. Most often, the king **inherited** the position from a family member, usually on his father's side. The king governed his own city-state. The people believed the king was god-like and could speak directly to the gods.

## ◄ Priests and Nobles ►

Below the chief priest were the other priests and nobles, who were generally wealthy. The priests and nobles organized **tribute** payments and religious festivals and ceremonies. In Aztec society, kings made warriors into nobles, if they showed great courage on the battlefield.

## Farmers ▶

Most Mesoamericans were farmers. Farmers' lives revolved around maize, or corn. If maize grew, the people could eat. If maize did not grow, the people would starve. Farmers were required to grow more maize than they could use themselves. The extra maize was used to pay tribute to the ruler of their city-state. The ruler would advise farmers when to plant crops and he arranged religious rituals and sacrifices to gain the favor of the gods, so crops would be plentiful. When they were not working the land, farmers worked on construction in the city. Farmers were also required to fight in wars.

## Slaves

Mesoamerican slaves were mainly captured warriors. In Aztec society, slaves were the lowest class of people but they did have some rights. Aztec slaves could save money and buy houses or land. Slaves could marry free Aztecs, and children born of these marriages were recognized as free people. If an Aztec slave escaped and ran fast enough to the ruler's palace without being caught by his owner, the slave could win his freedom.

◀ *Aztec merchants enjoyed status and wealth because traveling for trade was a difficult and dangerous job.*

# On the Menu

Maize was an important food for Mesoamericans. Maize kernels were removed from the cob and soaked overnight to soften. Often, a rock called limestone was added to the water to make the kernels more tender. The kernels were then ground with stones into meal and formed into a loaf. The loaf was cooked on top of a clay, three-pronged barbecue-like oven.

## A Woman's Place

Women were not accepted as the equal of men in Mesoamerica. Most women took care of the household, made meals and clothing, and cared for children. In a few royal families, a woman filled the role of ruler when the king was unable. Some royal and noble women also took part in ritual sacrifices of humans, and worked as healers, midwives, and priestesses.

## Clothing

Mesoamerican men wore loincloths, which were strips of cloth that wrapped around their waists and covered them to the tops of their thighs, and sleeveless capes. Women wore long cotton skirts with blouses. The use of color and feathers separated the wealthy nobles from the poorer people. Wealthy Mesoamericans could afford brighter designs on fine cotton. Farmers wore plain, white maguey cloth that was not as soft or ornate as cotton. Only nobles and kings wore elaborate headdresses, often made with the brilliant green tail feathers of the **sacred** quetzal bird.

*▲ Aztec girls were taught to cook and take care of the household.*

*▼ The clothing worn by Aztecs depended on their position in society. Only the wealthy wore bright cloth and colorful headdresses.*

## Here Comes the Bride

Mesoamericans usually married around the age of 20. The wedding ceremony took place at night and the bride was delivered to the groom on the back of an elderly woman. Instead of exchanging rings and kisses, the bride and groom tied their blouse and cloak together. Royal families of different city-states often married to strengthen ties between their communities.

## Homes and Palaces

Kings and emperors lived in stone palaces and temple-pyramids that still exist in places such as Tikal in Guatemala. Priests and nobles lived in homes made of adobe, or sun-dried clay, bricks. Most Mesoamericans lived in one-room homes with floors made of clay and covered with river sand. Family members slept on mats on the floor. Walls were made from canes or reeds, held up between wood posts. The spaces in between were filled with mud and then white-washed. Roofs were thatched, or covered with palm tree leaves.

▲ *An Aztec husband and wife tie their clothes together to symbolize their marriage.*

▼ *A simple Maya home was only one room.*

*thatched roof*

*cane or reeds*

# Blood Sacrifices

Ancient Mesoamericans worshiped many gods. They asked their gods to protect them from danger by making special offerings, called sacrifices. Sacrifices included flowers, vegetables, precious stones, and live animals. The Aztecs believed that they needed to make bloody human sacrifices to make the gods happy.

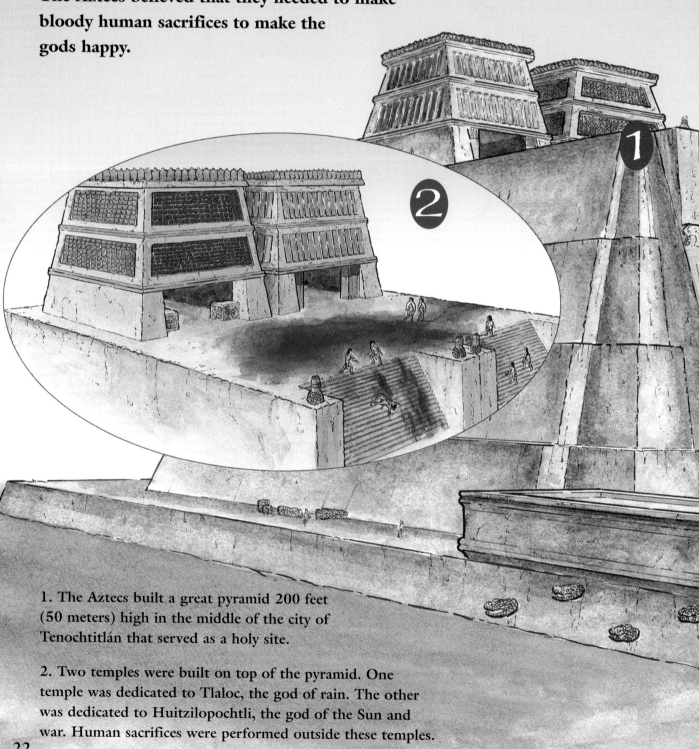

1. The Aztecs built a great pyramid 200 feet (50 meters) high in the middle of the city of Tenochtitlán that served as a holy site.

2. Two temples were built on top of the pyramid. One temple was dedicated to Tlaloc, the god of rain. The other was dedicated to Huitzilopochtli, the god of the Sun and war. Human sacrifices were performed outside these temples.

22

3. Human sacrifice victims were usually prisoners captured during battle. Priests held the victim over a flat stone. While the prisoner was still alive, another priest cut open his chest, took his heart out, and held it up to the sky.

4. A ceremonial knife made of obsidian or flint and decorated with jade was used by the priest to cut open the victim. Sometimes hundreds of human sacrifices were made in a day.

5. The dead bodies of sacrificed prisoners were thrown down the 113 steps of the pyramid onto a round stone at the bottom.

# Arts and Culture

Mesoamericans created art, sculpture, pottery, and architecture. Their art offers clues about their beliefs, fashions, and about what was important to the people. Most art and architecture from ancient Mesoamerica has been destroyed by time, the climate, or by human hands.

## Writing on the Wall

Around 300 A.D., Mesoamericans began creating large, rectangular stone panels called stelae. The stone panels outside temple-pyramids were carved to show rulers or high priests. Some carvings showed important historical events, such as great battles. Important women were sometimes shown in the carvings, elaborately dressed with large headdresses and jewelry. Accounts of the life and death of the person on the panel were written along the sides.

▲ *Painted murals on the walls of temples showed scenes from life in Mesoamerica. In this mural, musicians are shown playing turtle shell drums with a deer's antlers.*

## Hitting the High Notes

Mesoamericans were skilled musicians. The Maya made instruments out of turtle shells and gourds. Drums were also made by hollowing out logs, or from clay pots covered in animal skins. Small pottery figurines shaped like people, or sometimes half-animal, half-human creatures, were used as whistles.

◀ *Clay whistles made of bone and stone were played during religious ceremonies.*

## Precious Stones

Ancient Mesoamericans used precious stones such as jadeite, diopside, or serpentine as jewelry. Jade was often fashioned into masks or figurines for royal burials, containers for rituals, and jewelry for the wealthy.

## Body Beautiful

Ancient Mesoamericans pierced and tattooed their bodies to make themselves beautiful. They also filed their teeth to a point. The Maya changed the shape of their babies' skulls to resemble the Maize god's elongated head, which they considered beautiful. They did this by tying two boards to the front and back of infants' heads for several days after birth. The Maya also pierced ears with large earrings. They made tattoo-like scars on their bodies with paint made from crushed flowers and insects.

▲ *Jade masks were often placed over the faces of nobles when they died.*

# The Game of Champions

Throughout Mesoamerica, a ball game associated with both religion and war was played. The object of the game was to get a rubber ball through a stone ring on the side of the court wall. A player wore paddles at the sides of his waist which he used to hit the ball. Both Maya and Aztec art depicts losing teams being sacrificed. Rulers played the ball game against their captives to decide who would live and who would die. The rulers always won. Losers had their heads cut off at the end of the game.

◀ *A statue shows a ballplayer wearing padding for protection.*

# Science in the Sky

**The ancient Mesoamericans studied the stars in the night sky believing they held the answers to their questions. They also studied the human body and learned how to make medicine from plants.**

## Star Gazing

Ancient Maya astronomers studied the stars and predicted solar and **lunar** eclipses, the cycles of the planet Venus, and the movements of the **constellations**. The Maya believed that these occurrences were caused by the gods. When constructing temples, builders made sure they lined up with the sun and stars. At Chichén Itzá, the main Maya city in the Yucatán peninsula, there is a pyramid dedicated to Quetzalcoatl, the Feathered Serpent God. At the spring and autumn **equinoxes**, the sun gradually shines on the pyramid's stairs and the serpent head at its base. This creates the image of a snake slithering down the sacred mountain to earth.

▼ *The Carocol, at the ancient Maya city of Chichén Itzá, Mexico, is believed to be an observatory.* **Some of its doors and windows line up with the orbit of planets.**

26

## Medicine

Maya and Aztec healers wrote about medicines that came from plants. To soothe a sore throat, a healer advised the patient to sip thickened maguey syrup. Aztec physicians used obsidian blades to cut open sores or made a cut near a swelled body part to let the patient bleed. The wound was then stitched up again using a cactus spine as a needle and hair as thread.

▲ *An Aztec healer cares for a broken skull.*

## Textile Making

Weaving fabric for clothing and other uses was the job of Maya and Aztec women. The first step was to prepare fiber either from a plant or animal. Ancient weavers spun thread themselves by hand. They used a technology of spindles and whorls. A spindle was a stick-like thread holder. As the weaver twisted fiber into thread, she wound it around the spindle. A whorl, a circular part with a hole in the middle, was attached to the base of the spindle. It provided weight to steady the spindle in its spinning motion. Whorls were made of carved wood or pottery. Weavers colored fabric with a dye made from dried, crushed bugs and plants.

▶ *For weaving, women used backstrap looms which are still used today. One end of the loom was tied to a tree or wall and the other end was tied to the weaver's waist. The weaver leaned back to keep the threads tight as she worked.*

Archaeologists know that some Mesoamerican cities were abandoned or destroyed. They do not know the reason why. Some think the land surrounding the cities was over farmed and could no longer grow crops to feed the population, forcing the people to move. Others believe the cities were attacked by invaders or even by rebels within the cities.

## The Fall of the Olmec

The building of one of the greatest Olmec cities, near present-day San Lorenzo, Mexico, began in 1700 B.C. Workers built a massive platform of earth and clay, shaped like a bird flying. The city had colossal head sculptures and other heavy art objects that must have required massive human effort to sculpt, all without the use of metal tools or wheeled carts. Around 1200 B.C., archaeologists believe that the city workers either rebelled against their rulers, or that the city was invaded by outsiders. They believe this because a clay and earth bird platform was unfinished and abandoned, and the city's great sculptures and art were deliberately vandalized.

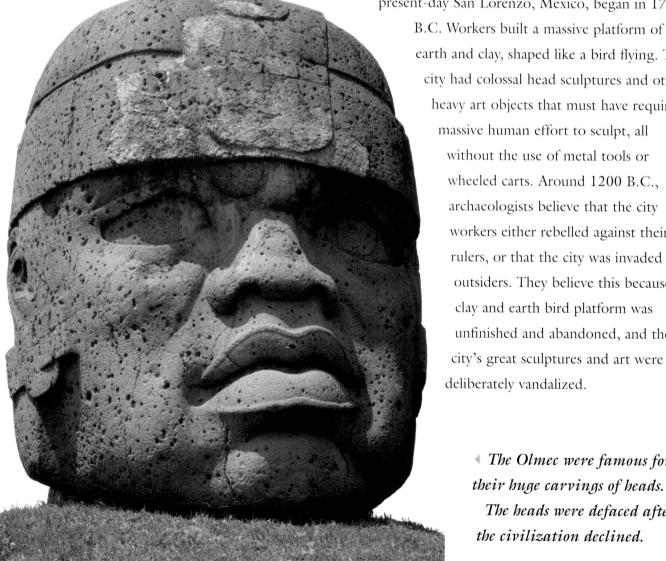

◄ *The Olmec were famous for their huge carvings of heads. The heads were defaced after the civilization declined.*

*The Pyramid of the Sun in the city of Teotihuacán became a sacred site to the Aztec many centuries after Teotihuacán's collapse.*

*On one side of the Great Plaza of the Mayan city of Tikal stood the Temple of the Giant Jaguar. The 145 foot (44 meter) tall temple was believed to be the passageway to the underworld, where rulers went after death.*

## Teotihuacan

In its day, Teotihuacán was the largest and grandest city in ancient Mesoamerica. It was thought to be the place where the gods were made. In 500 A.D., from 125,000 to 200,000 people lived there. Teotihuacán was the home of the largest and most famous pyramid-temples, the Pyramid of the Sun and the Pyramid of the Moon. Obsidian mines found north of the city added to the city's wealth. Around 600 A.D., the city of Teotihuacán began to decline. A severe drought that ruined crops is thought to have led to its downfall. Archaeologists believe the city may have been attacked in 725 A.D., or been the site of a rebellion. Evidence shows all the city's buildings and art were destroyed in the attack.

# Spanish Conquest

**In 1519, Spanish explorer Hernán Cortés sailed to the coast of Mexico with 500 soldiers. Cortés was in search of gold for himself and his king. The search for gold ended with the Conquest of the Aztec Empire.**

◀ *Aztec emperor Motecuhzoma welcomed Cortés and his men to Tenochtitlán. Motecuhzoma believed that Cortés was the god Quetzalcoatl.*

## Bad Omens

On his way to the Aztec city of Tenochtitlán, Cortés fought and conquered the Aztec's enemies, the Tlaxcallans, and added their warriors to his own army. He marched to Tenochtitlán and met Aztec emperor Motecuhzoma on November 8, 1519. Motecuhzoma thought Cortés was the god Quetzalcoatl, whom legend said would one day return, and invited the Spanish leader and his army to rest at his palace. Cortés and his men were uneasy about staying there, and decided to hold Motecuhzoma hostage so the Aztecs would not harm them.

▶ *Hernán Cortés conquered the Aztecs in 1521.*

## Death of Motecuhzoma

When Cortés was called away on a military matter, he took 100 soldiers with him and left the rest at Motecuhzoma's palace. Cortés returned to find his men in trouble and forced Motecuhzoma to talk the Aztecs out of fighting. The Aztecs threw rocks at Motecuhzoma. When he died a few days later, the Spanish said that the rocks thrown by the Aztecs had killed the ruler, but the Aztecs maintained that Motecuhzoma was strangled by the Spanish. The cause of Motecuhzoma's death remains a mystery today.

## How the Spanish Won

On July 1, 1520, Cortés and his men tried to sneak out of Tenochtitlán but were spotted by Aztec warriors. During a battle, called The Night of Sorrow, over 4,000 men of the Spanish and Tlaxcallan army were killed. Cortés and some of his men managed to escape. With new troops, both Spanish and Tlaxcallan, Cortés built ships to attack the island city of Tenochtitlán. With 16,000 men, Cortés attacked one more time, in May, 1521. In the end, the Aztec were defeated. The Spanish demolished Tenochtitlán and built Mexico City in its place.

▲ *Protected by armor and carrying more powerful weapons than the Aztecs, the Spanish were able to defeat the Aztecs and conquer the empire.*

# Glossary

**alliance** A partnership between peoples or countries

**archaeologist** A person who studies past human life as shown by fossil relics, monuments, and tools left by ancient peoples

**astronomical** Of or relating to the study of the stars and planets

**canal** An artificial waterway for boats or for draining or irrigating land

**carnivore** Meat eater

**climate** The usual weather of a place

**coincide** To happen at the same time or place

**conquer** To get or gain by armed force

**constellation** A group of stars that form patterns

**dense** Close or crowded together

**descendant** A person who can trace his or her family roots to a certain family group

**empire** One political unit that occupies a large region of land and is governed by one ruler

**equinox** The two times each year in Spring and Fall when the sun appears overhead at the equator, and the day and night are of equal length

**estuary** A place where the sea meets a river

**ferment** To allow a substance to change over time, usually into a new product, such as alcohol

**fertilize** To apply a substance, such as ash or manure, which helps plants grow

**humidity** The amount of moisture in the air

**inherit** To receive money or property after someone's death

**isthmus** A narrow strip of land that connects two other larger land areas

**lunar** Having to do with the moon

**noble** An important person of high rank or born into a wealthy family

**nomadic** Moving from place to place rather than settling in one location

**observatory** A specially built structure for studying objects in the sky

**orbit** The path taken by one body around another, such as the Earth's orbit around the sun

**peninsula** Land that is surrounded on three sides by water

**sacred** Having special religious meaning

**sacrifice** An act of offering something to God or a god, such as flowers or precious stones, and can involve killing a human being or animal in a religious ceremony

**solar** Having to do with the sun

**stucco** Plaster used to cover outside walls or decorate inside walls

**symbolize** Something that represents something else.

**tribute** A payment made by one ruler or nation to another to show obedience or to obtain peace or protection

**whitewashed** Whitened with a mix of water and lime

# Index

architecture 24
astronomy 26
Aztec 4, 5, 6, 8, 10, 11, 17, 18, 19, 20, 31

ball game 25

Calakmul 9
calendars 17
Chichén Itzá 26
children 10
city-states 8, 9, 13
clothing 20
Cortés, Hernan
Costa Rica 6

farming 8, 12, 18, 19
Flower Wars 11

Guatemala 6, 14, 15

Gulf of Mexico 5

Honduras 6
Huitzilopochtli 10

jaguars 7

language 14

marriage
mathematics 16
Maya 4, 5, 6, 8, 14, 15, 16, 17, 24, 25, 26, 29
medicine 27
Mexico 6, 26, 30
Mexico City 31
money 13
Motecuhzoma 30, 31
music 24

Nicaragua 6
Night of Sorrow 31

Olmec 4, 5, 6, 7, 8, 14, 28

Pacal 9
Palenque 9
Panama 6
Popol Vuh 15
pottery 24
priests 18, 19

Quetzalcoatl 30

San Lorenzo 28
sculpture 24
Sierra Madre (mountains) 6
slaves 8, 11, 19
Spanish 5, 10, 15, 17, 30, 31

Tenochtitlán 10, 13, 18, 30, 31
Teotihuacán 29
textiles 27
Tikal 9, 14
Tlacelel 10, 11
Toltecs 5
trade 13
Triple Alliance 10

volcanoes 6, 7

war 10, 11
wildlife 7
women 20, 21
writing 14, 24

Zapotecs 5